STAR SIGNS

REVEAL THE SECRETS OF THE ZODIAC

Published in 2021 by Mortimer Children's Books

An Imprint of Welbeck Children's Limited, part of Welbeck Publishing Group.

20 Mortimer Street London W1T 3JW

Text & Illustrations © Welbeck Children's Limited, part of Welbeck Publishing Group.

Designed and packaged by: Dynamo Limited
Written by: Sara Stanford
Art editor: Deborah Vickers
Editor: Jenni Lazell

ISBN 978-1-83935-096-2

Printed in Dubai

10 9 8 7 6 5 4 3 2 1

STAR SIGNS

REVEAL THE SECRETS OF THE ZODIAC

MORTIMER

CONTENTS

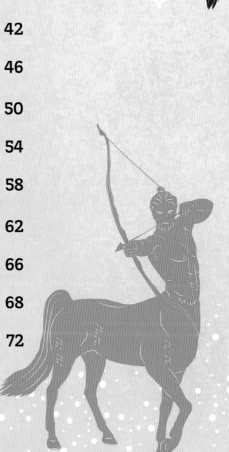

Western
ASTROLOGY

Astrology is the study of how planets and stars affect the way people behave. Astrologers believe each zodiac sign or star sign has certain characteristics, for example—Leos are bright and lively and Scorpios can be secretive. In western astrology, the zodiac is split equally into twelve different signs. There is a zodiac sign for each month of the year and each sign has its own name and symbol.

ZODIAC FACT

"Zodiac" comes from a Latin word that means "circle of animals."

ZODIAC FACT

Each zodiac sign has its own color, that has a special meaning for that sign.

FIND YOUR STAR SIGN

YOUR BIRTHDAY	YOUR SIGN
MARCH 21–APRIL 19	Aries
APRIL 20–MAY 20	Taurus
MAY 21–JUNE 20	Gemini
JUNE 21–JULY 22	Cancer
JULY 23–AUGUST 22	Leo
AUGUST 23–SEPTEMBER 22	Virgo
SEPTEMBER 23–OCTOBER 22	Libra
OCTOBER 23–NOVEMBER 21	Scorpio
NOVEMBER 22–DECEMBER 21	Sagittarius
DECEMBER 22–JANUARY 19	Capricorn
JANUARY 20–FEBRUARY 18	Aquarius
FEBRUARY 19–MARCH 20	Pisces

Turn to page 66 to find out about Eastern astrology!

History of
WESTERN ASTROLOGY

People have been looking at the stars and planets as guides for thousands of years. Ancient civilizations believed in many gods who lived in the sky among the stars and planets. These gods controlled the destiny of humans.

STAR GODS

In the Ancient Babylonian civilization, people believed that by watching the movement of the stars and planets they could find out how the gods were going to behave. To make it easier to keep track of the stars, they divided them into 12 constellations that they named after their gods, and these became the 12 zodiac signs. Later, the Ancient Greeks used their knowledge of mathematics to bring more order and understanding to the movement of the constellations in the sky. The Ancient Greeks kept many of the Babylonian myths but named the constellations after Greek gods. This was passed on to the Ancient Romans, who gave their own names to the constellations, and this has become the zodiac that we use today.

SKY GAZING

People began to spot patterns in what was happening in the sky and on Earth. For example, in spring and summer, when the sky was light and the Sun warm, plants grew, and in winter, when the Sun was cold and the days dark, plants died. So farmers began to use the sky to predict what would happen to their crops and animals. Kings and rulers had special advisors who would read the sky and predict events for them, such as if a battle would be successful. Soon people were using the stars to predict all sorts of things, such as the best time to get married or begin a journey.

In Ancient Greece the first day of spring was considered the beginning of the year, as this is when new growth started. This was the time when the Sun appeared in the constellation of Aries, so the zodiac begins in April, with the sign of Aries.

MOON MAGIC

In ancient times the shape of the Moon was very important in predicting what was going to happen. The shape of the Moon is still very important in astrology today.

MOON PHASE AND MEANING

NEW MOON
New start

CRESCENT MOON
New ideas, learning new things

FIRST QUARTER MOON
New growth, achieving your goals

GIBBOUS MOON
Trying to perfect things in your life

FULL MOON
Working with others

DISSEMINATING MOON
Finishing projects

LAST QUARTER MOON
Preparing for new projects or hobbies

BALSAMIC MOON
Moving on, looking forward to the new

CONSTELLATIONS

Constellations are stars grouped together to create shapes in the sky. These groups of stars are visible from Earth and include animals, beings from Greek myths, and objects. Each star sign has its very own constellation. These zodiac constellations form a path. The Moon, Sun, and planets all continuously pass through this path. Astrologers then look at the positions within this pathway to make their zodiac forecasts.

ARIES   TAURUS   GEMINI   CANCER

LEO

VIRGO

LIBRA

SCORPIO

SAGITTARIUS

CAPRICORN

AQUARIUS

PISCES

OPHIUCHUS

There are 12 constellations for the 12 months of the year. Ophiuchus (oh-few-kuss) is the 13th constellation of the zodiac, but it is not technically a star sign as it is not matched with a month. In Greek, Ophiuchus means "serpent-bearer."

STAR FACT

The biggest constellation is called Hydra. The smallest constellation is called Crux.

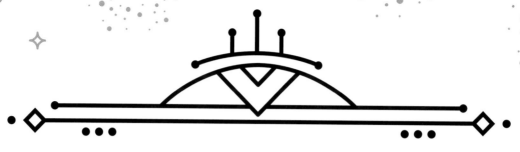

Which Element
ARE YOU?

Each star sign is ruled by an element. The elements are: Air, Water, Fire, and Earth. Each element has certain characteristics that rule the star sign it is associated with. The elements also show how well different signs go together—for example, Earth and Water signs are well matched.

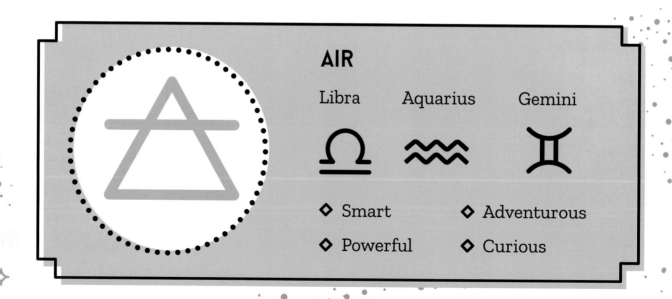

AIR

Libra   Aquarius   Gemini

◇ Smart   ◇ Adventurous

◇ Powerful   ◇ Curious

EARTH

Virgo ♍ Capricorn ♑ Taurus ♉

◇ Reliable
◇ Trustworthy
◇ Down-to-earth
◇ Practical

WATER

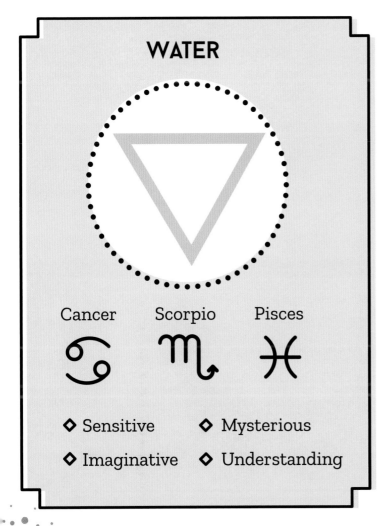

Cancer ♋ Scorpio ♏ Pisces ♓

◇ Sensitive
◇ Imaginative
◇ Mysterious
◇ Understanding

FIRE

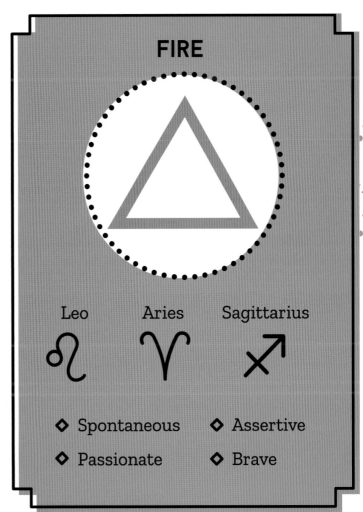

Leo ♌ Aries ♈ Sagittarius ♐

◇ Spontaneous
◇ Passionate
◇ Assertive
◇ Brave

Ruling
PLANETS

Astrologers believe that each planet has its own set of characteristics. Every star sign has a ruling planet, and this planet has the most influence over the sign's personality and behavior. Some planets rule two signs—for example, Mercury rules Virgo and Gemini. Although ruling planets are the most powerful in each zodiac sign, all the planets are important, depending on their position in the sky.

☉ SUN

The Sun is what shapes your sense of who you are.

◇ The Sun is the star that is closest to Earth

◇ Helios is the Sun god in Greek mythology

☾ MOON

The Moon is all about your mood, and how you deal with your feelings.

◆ You only ever see one side of the Moon—the other side is always turned away from Earth

◆ Selene is the goddess of the Moon

☿ MERCURY

Mercury affects how you understand and how you learn.

◆ Mercury is the smallest planet in the Solar System

◆ In mythology Mercury is the messenger god and has winged sandals

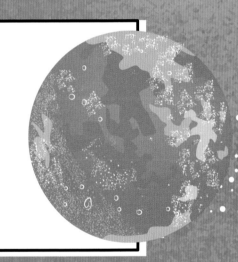

♀ VENUS

This planet affects the way you care for others and yourself.

◆ Venus is the hottest planet in the Solar System

◆ Venus is the Roman goddess of love and beauty—in Greek mythology she is called Aphrodite

♃ JUPITER

This planet is all about hope and growth.

◆ The largest planet in our Solar System

◆ Jupiter is the King of the gods and is called Zeus in Greek mythology

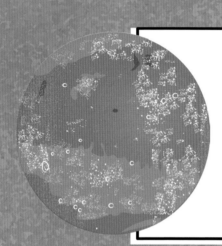

♂ MARS

Mars is all about your need to succeed and do well.

◆ Mars is also called the "Red Planet"

◆ In mythology Mars is the fiery god of war

♄ SATURN

This planet is about how you behave when faced with difficult situations.

◆ Saturn has 150 moons

◆ Saturn is also known as Cronus, the god of time in Greek mythology

♅ URANUS

Uranus is the planet of unexpected change and doing things that are unplanned.

◆ Uranus is the coldest planet in the Solar System

◆ In Greek mythology Uranus represents Heaven

♆ NEPTUNE

Neptune is the planet of dreams, healing, and intuition.

◆ Neptune is the planet farthest away from the Sun

◆ Neptune is the sea god and is called Poseidon
   in Greek mythology

♇ PLUTO

This planet deals with rebirth and transformation.

◆ The surface of Pluto is rocky and icy

◆ Pluto is the Roman god of the Underworld,
   called Hades in Greek mythology

ARIES
The Ram

Aries are bursting with creativity and always put 100 percent into anything they do. They are fearless when it comes to tackling challenges, and are always determined to be the best they can.

ZODIAC FACT

In the zodiac, Aries is the first astrological sign.

ARIES ARE ...

◆ Ambitious

◆ Cheerful

◆ Versatile

FAMOUS ARIES

◆ Alex Wassabi

◆ Vincent van Gogh

◆ Emma Watson

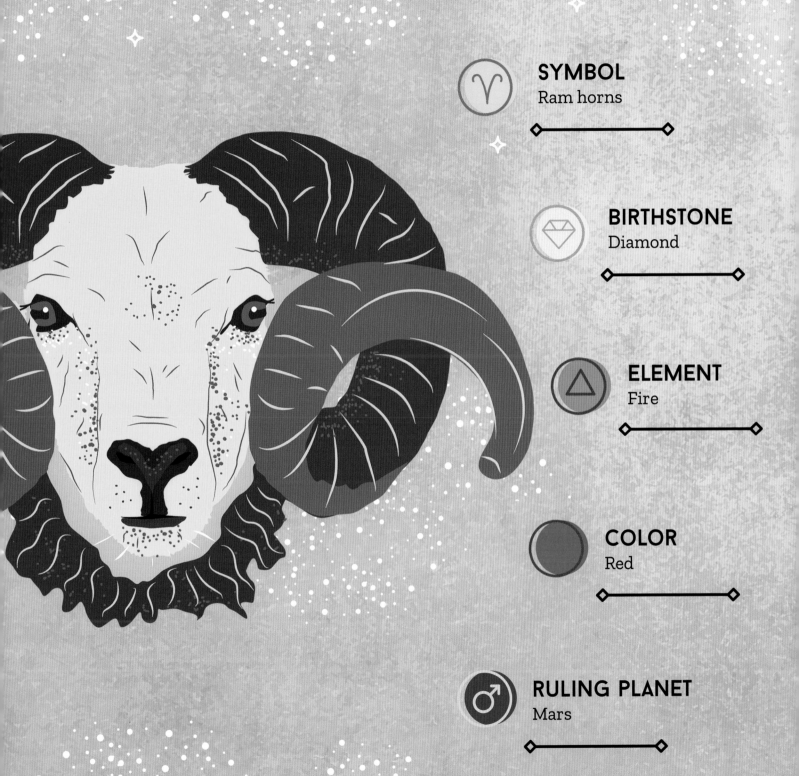

SYMBOL
Ram horns

BIRTHSTONE
Diamond

ELEMENT
Fire

COLOR
Red

RULING PLANET
Mars

ALL ABOUT ♈ ARIES

HEAD OF THE HERD

Being independent and fearless helps make Aries strong personalities. They are not afraid to speak their minds and say what they think. Aries are high achievers and have a go-getter attitude. Why waste time thinking about it when you could just make it happen, right? Each star sign is influenced by the one that went before it—however, Aries has no sign before it to learn from. This is why some Aries tend to leap before they look and are more likely to start a project without first thinking things through.

STAR ADVICE

Take your time

BUTTING HEADS

Aries are impulsive. They are always on the go and they move very fast! Aries can become impatient if they feel that other people are holding them back. So, do your best to keep up. It's no surprise that Aries can clash with Capricorns, who like to plan every last detail. Aries are natural leaders and they may struggle if others try to step on their toes. Aries can find their friends and soul mates among Geminis. A Gemini's open and carefree nature is more likely to go along with an Aries' madcap plan.

LIKES

◇ Leading

◇ Spontaneity

◇ Sports

DISLIKES

◇ Being told what to do

ARIES FRIENDS

Although Aries are outspoken and strong-minded, they are sensitive souls. If you're good to them, they will be good to you. When it comes to disagreements, this star sign doesn't often start arguments. Just be sure to stay on their good side!

COMPATIBLE SIGNS

Gemini

Leo

SCHOOL REPORT

Aries students will dive into new projects and want to try everything school has to offer. They have tons of energy, so they can take on lots of different things at the same time. Boredom is their enemy, so they need to keep busy. Others might tell them to slow down, but Aries like to keep moving!

ZODIAC FACT

There are 42 constellations that represent animals and Aries the Ram is one of them!

GOOD TO KNOW

Aries are fitness fanatics. They will join in all the sports and exercise groups they can, from trampolining to charity runs. They are very competitive in everything they do and expect the same high standards from other players.

APRIL 20–MAY 20

TAURUS
The Bull

Cooking, gardening, and good music are just a few things that make a Taurus tick. People of this star sign are known for being patient and practical. They are super organized and persistent, so once a Taurus makes a plan, they REALLY like to stick to it.

TAUREANS ARE ...

◆ Reliable

◆ Practical

◆ Patient

FAMOUS TAUREANS

◆ Gigi Hadid

◆ Mark Zuckerberg

◆ Dwayne Johnson

ZODIAC FACT

Being outdoors and close to nature is important to a Taurus.

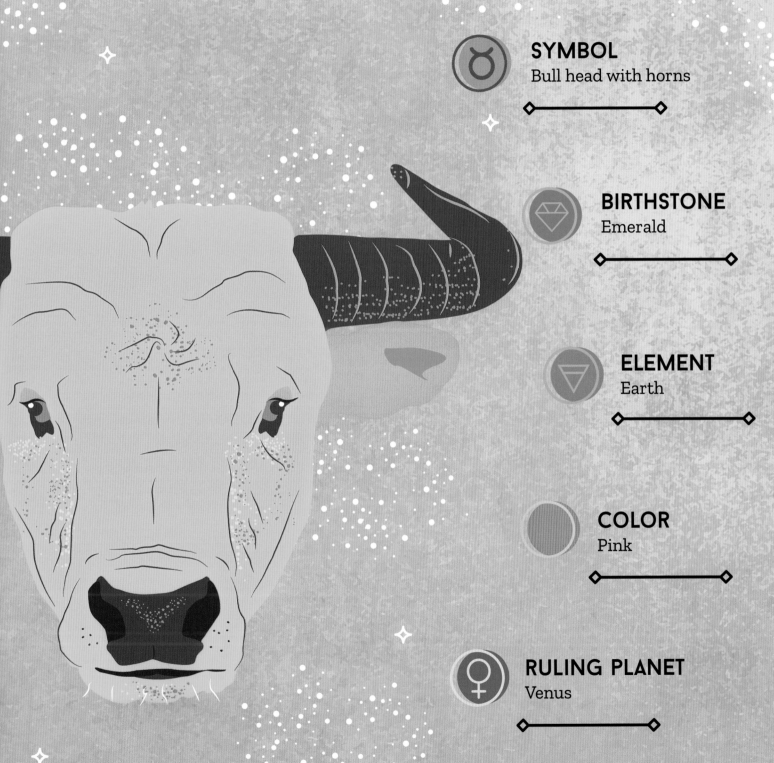

SYMBOL
Bull head with horns

BIRTHSTONE
Emerald

ELEMENT
Earth

COLOR
Pink

RULING PLANET
Venus

ALL ABOUT

♉ TAURUS

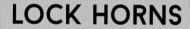

UNFLAPPA-BULL

Calm and organized, Taureans enjoy taking care of people and make truly loyal friends. As well as being devoted to those they care about, Taureans are patient and level-headed. All this makes a Taurus someone you can rely on in a tricky situation for practical help and a supportive hug! Taureans are very loyal, whether it be to a friend or a plan of action. They like to see things through and enjoy the satisfaction that finishing a project brings.

LOCK HORNS

Taureans don't adapt well to sudden changes, which can make them seem stubborn. They are extremely practical and like to do things the right way, even if this means something takes twice as long. This can often upset the people around them, but a Taurus will always believe they are in the right. Appearance is a big deal for a Taurus. They always take plenty of time getting ready for anything, from a trip to the movies to a school field trip.

STAR ADVICE
Try new things

24

LIKES

- ◇ Luxury
- ◇ Cooking
- ◇ Music

DISLIKES

- ◇ Changes being made to their plans

TAURUS FRIENDS

People enjoy spending time with Taureans. They are kind, loyal, and generous, and because of this they have lots of friends. As well as socializing with their friends and family, Taureans love to just relax and enjoy time by themselves.

ZODIAC FACT

Taurus lucky numbers are 1 and 9.

COMPATIBLE SIGNS

Cancer

Virgo

GOOD TO KNOW

Taureans have strong voices, so they make great singers. They also have the staying power and patience to practice, practice, practice, until they get it right. They love to sing with friends or in a more formal choir or group.

SCHOOL REPORT

Taurus students like to do things slowly and steadily. Taureans like routine and fit right in with school schedules. They enjoy school activities such as crafts, art, music, and dance.

GEMINI
The Twins

People with this star sign may be deep thinkers, but they manage to balance this with being fun and sociable, too! Geminis are great at getting along with people and make friends with whoever they meet. Making plans for parties, outings and other fun activities is heaven for lively Geminis.

ZODIAC FACT

The number 5 represents communication, which is why it's Gemini's lucky number.

GEMINIS ARE ...

◆ Adaptable

◆ Talkative

◆ Creative

FAMOUS GEMINIS

◆ Iggy Azalea

◆ Emma Chamberlain

◆ Bear Grylls

SYMBOL
Roman numeral 2

BIRTHSTONE
Pearl

ELEMENT
Air

COLOR
Green

RULING PLANET
Mercury

ALL ABOUT GEMINI

DOUBLE THE FUN

Meet the smart, witty and fun twins of the zodiac! Want to know what you get if you mix curiosity with brains? A Gemini—also known as the ideal quiz teammate, because they know loads of stuff! Geminis have lots of great ideas, as well as being easygoing and open-minded. Geminis love new experiences and aren't afraid to try almost anything. They can make friends feel good just by being with them. All in all, Geminis are fabulous people to have around.

ZODIAC FACT

Gemini is a mutable sign. These signs are understanding and flexible.

STAR ADVICE

Listen to friends

KEEPING UP

This star sign is usually very balanced so finding fault is difficult. They can constantly change their plans, which can be annoying for others. Because Geminis are mega curious and interested in the next big thing, their friends do not always have their full attention. Also, a Gemini might not realize when they have upset someone.

LIKES

◆ Chatting

◆ Books

◆ Music

DISLIKES

◆ Being alone

GEMINI FRIENDS

Social butterflies, Geminis are good friends to have around! They hate being alone and are always on the lookout for things to do. Boredom is something that Geminis dread—they need to have lots of entertainment.

CONSTELLATION

Gemini means "twins" in Latin. The constellation is named after Castor and Pollux from Greek mythology. The two brightest stars are said to represent their heads.

GOOD TO KNOW

Geminis enjoy being with people and love to learn, so they are really into games and competitive quizzes. They are really good at remembering facts, so choose a Gemini as a teammate if you are competing in a general knowledge quiz.

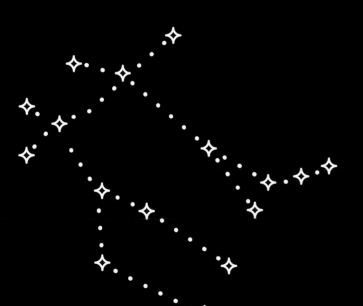

COMPATIBLE SIGNS

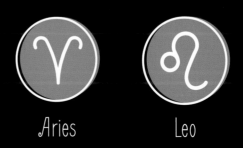

Aries   Leo

CANCER

The Crab

Once you are friends with Cancers, you have their trust forever. Sensitive, loving and caring, people with this star sign can be daydreamers. They are strongly influenced by their emotions and often need a lot of support from family and friends.

ZODIAC FACT

In Greek mythology, a giant crab attacked Hercules as he was fighting the many-headed sea monster, Hydra.

CANCERS ARE ...

◆ Loyal

◆ Trustworthy

◆ Caring

FAMOUS CANCERS

◆ Priyanka Chopra

◆ Elon Musk

◆ Frida Kahlo

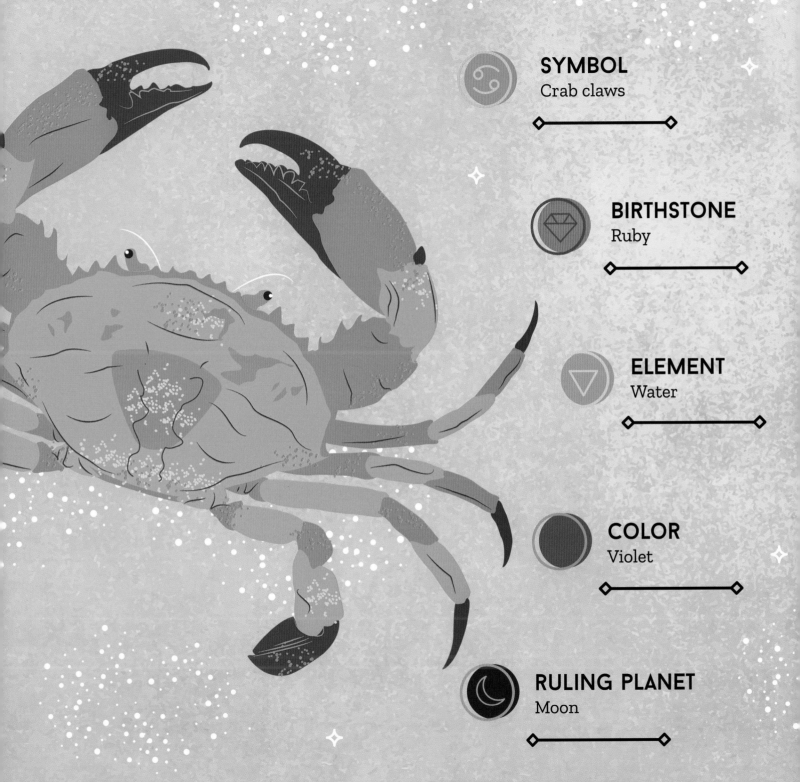

SYMBOL
Crab claws

BIRTHSTONE
Ruby

ELEMENT
Water

COLOR
Violet

RULING PLANET
Moon

ALL ABOUT CANCER

CREATIVE AND KIND

Loyal Cancers have a wonderful imagination and a special way of looking at things. They certainly make the world more interesting! Cancer is a naturally sympathetic star sign, and this quality makes them a great friend. They are also reliable and work hard to complete any task at home or at school. Cancers are brilliantly creative. They love to write, paint, and do crafts. You are lucky if you have a Cancer as a teacher, as they are open-minded, kind, and caring.

STAR ADVICE
Trust your feelings

GETTING CRABBY

Having a Cancer friend is sometimes difficult, as Cancer folk expect a lot from their friends. Cancers can be unpredictable in their actions and can have negative thoughts if things don't go their way. Cancers are sometimes insecure, so they often need people around to reassure them of how great they are. If you are unlucky enough to catch them on a bad day, you might witness their mood swings, when they can turn sulky and stubborn.

LIKES

◇ Art

◇ Being near or in water

◇ Spending time with family and friends

DISLIKES

◇ Being criticized

ZODIAC FACT

Number 7 is linked to the Moon, which rules this sign!

COMPATIBLE SIGNS

Capricorn   Taurus

CANCER FRIENDS

Family and home are everything to this star sign. They are much happier being with one close friend rather than a huge group. This star sign can be insecure and sensitive to criticism, so friends need to be careful what they say.

SCHOOL REPORT

Cancers work hard in school and are polite and respectful, but they may start daydreaming in class! It can take them a little while to get to know their classmates well.

GOOD TO KNOW

In astrology, Cancers are more likely to go for a dog than a cat as a pet. They love to take care of their pets and their pup will love all the attention. A cat is just a bit too independent for a caring Cancer.

LEO

The Lion

Leos are strong and confident people who are known for being kind and caring. They are also honest and super dedicated to their friendships. Leos love entertaining people, which makes them popular and loads of fun to be around!

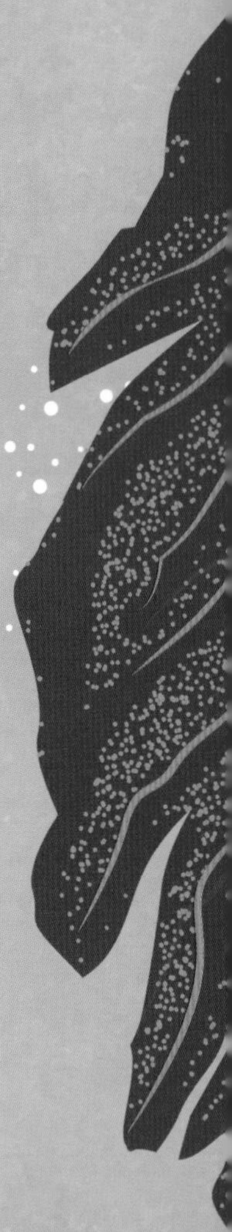

ZODIAC FACT

Sunflowers are linked to Leos.

LEOS ARE ...

◊ Funny

◊ Loyal

◊ Confident

FAMOUS LEOS

◊ Jason Momoa

◊ Meghan Markle

◊ J. K. Rowling

SYMBOL
Lion head and mane

BIRTHSTONE
Peridot

ELEMENT
Fire

COLOR
Gold

RULING PLANET
Sun

ALL ABOUT ♌ LEO

THE MANE EVENT

Leos are creative, generous, and big-hearted. There is nothing that Leos enjoy more than being in the spotlight. They love sparkle and glitter and never settle for anything but the best. Fun-loving Leos enjoy performing, socializing, and helping others. Leos like to be the best at everything they do. They are outspoken and say what they think. If Leos are upset they say what they have to and move on. Leos are often the leaders in their own group of friends. People with this star sign are happiest when they are with friends or family having a good time.

> **STAR ADVICE**
> Be still and breathe!

A LION'S PRIDE

Although Leos are known for having plenty of energy, if they don't want to do something, they'll be sure to let you know about it and find a way out of it. Plus, Leos can be a little stubborn when it suits them. Their love of leadership makes it no surprise that they dislike being told what to do. Leos can find it difficult not to be in control, whether it's making weekend plans or having a party, especially if they disagree with the person who is in charge.

LIKES

◆ Bright colors

◆ Music

◆ Fun

DISLIKES

◆ Not being the center of attention

ZODIAC FACT

1, 4, and 6 are lucky numbers for Leos.

CONSTELLATION

The Leo constellation is one of the easiest to recognize because it is one of the only constellations that looks like what it is called—Leo means "lion" in Latin. For the easiest way to find Leo, look for the Big Dipper.

LEO FRIENDS

Once you are friends with a Leo, you are friends for life! Leos are incredibly loyal. It can take a while to become friends in the first place, but if you are patient, it will be worth it. Leos tend to get on well with other fire signs like Aries and Sagittarius, but clash with Capricorn or Pisces.

COMPATIBLE SIGNS

Aries

Sagittarius

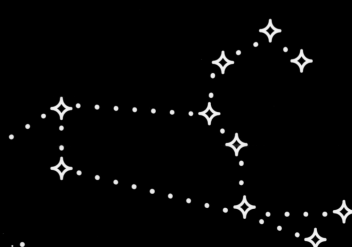

VIRGO
The Maiden

The cool, calm and steady Virgo never gives in to pressure. They are logical, clear thinkers who think before they act, making them a good person to have around in a crisis. Virgos take pride in their amazing memory and have a sharp eye for detail, too.

VIRGOS ARE ...

- ◆ Good with details
- ◆ Calm under pressure
- ◆ Practical

FAMOUS VIRGOS

- ◆ Jesse Owens
- ◆ Beyoncé
- ◆ Sunita Williams

ZODIAC FACT

Wednesday is the luckiest day of the week for Virgos.

SYMBOL
Intestines

BIRTHSTONE
Blue sapphire

ELEMENT
Earth

COLOR
Bottle green

RULING PLANET
Mercury

39

ALL ABOUT  VIRGO

THE THINKERS

Nature-loving, modest and always polite—there are a lot of things to like about Virgos. They are hardworking and they love making themselves useful—they get a real kick out of helping others. Virgos want everything to be perfect, and for this reason they take their time before starting any project. However, when they do get started, you can be sure they will put their heart and soul into it.

STAR ADVICE
Relax and have fun

GOT TO BE PERFECT

Being a total perfectionist does have its downsides. Virgos are always striving to be the best, so they can put themselves under a lot of pressure and worry about making mistakes. Their friends and family can sometimes run out of patience, as Virgos check everything over and over again. Being the center of attention also makes Virgos nervous—they prefer to stay in the background.

LIKES

◆ Nature

◆ Reading

◆ Everything in its place

DISLIKES

◆ Needing to ask people for help

COMPATIBLE SIGNS

Taurus

Scorpio

SCHOOL REPORT

Virgos study hard, are neat and deliver homework on time. They love doing research and will take the time to really get into a subject. They take pride in their schoolwork and treat teachers and fellow students with respect.

VIRGO FRIENDS

Virgos are incredibly loyal friends, but being best buddies with one can have its challenges. For example, their need to be perfect can make them critical of those who are less than perfect. Finding someone who shares the same interests and hobbies is the most important thing for a Virgo.

GOOD TO KNOW

There is a lot of mystery about the meaning of the symbol for Virgo. Some experts think the sign stands for the letter M, and that the bit attached to it is like a tail wrapped around itself. This is meant to symbolize the control Virgos have over themsleves and what they do. Some think Virgo's curving symbol stands for intestines. This sign tends to worry a lot about their health.

ZODIAC FACT

Virgo is often said to represent Persephone, the goddess of the harvest in Greek mythology.

LIBRA
The Scales

Libras are gentle people with loads of charm and a great sense of humor. This sign can strike up a conversation with just about anyone and is super likable. Libras hate chaos, and they are the most balanced and fair in the zodiac.

ZODIAC FACT

Libras love bluebells and roses.

LIBRAS ARE ...

◇ Charming

◇ Tactful

◇ Peaceful

FAMOUS LIBRAS

◇ Serena Williams

◇ Zac Efron

◇ Brie Larson

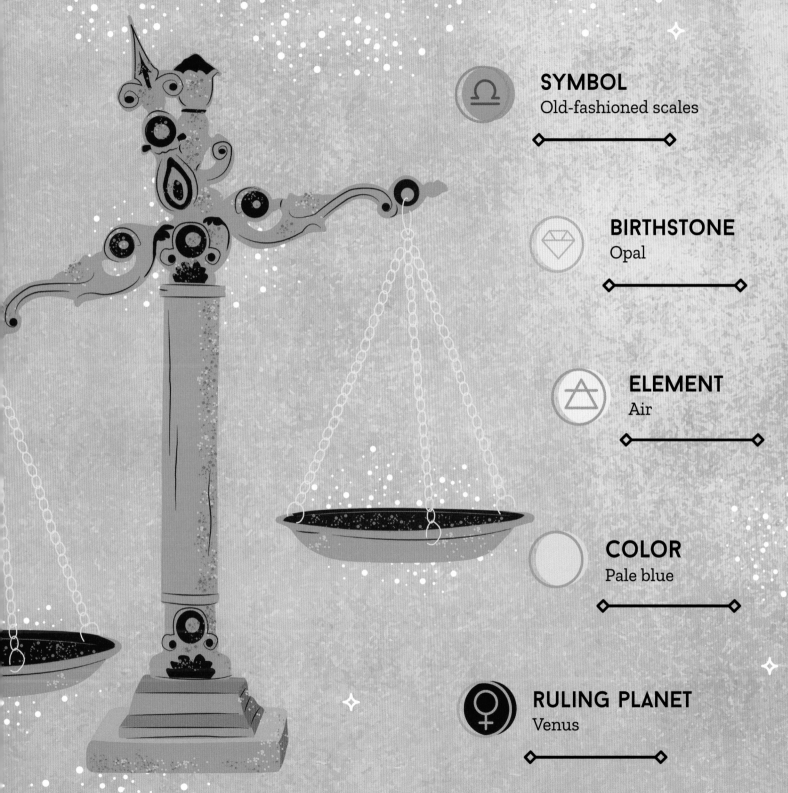

SYMBOL
Old-fashioned scales

BIRTHSTONE
Opal

ELEMENT
Air

COLOR
Pale blue

RULING PLANET
Venus

ALL ABOUT ♎ LIBRA

ALL IS FAIR

It is all about fairness for this star sign. Libras are great listeners because they are genuinely interested in hearing everyone's opinion. If you are going to have an argument with anyone, make it a Libra, as they weigh up each side equally. This sociable star sign is probably still in touch with their friends from preschool! They put in ALL the effort to keep friendships alive. They are wonderful to have in your life!

STAR ADVICE
Trust yourself

ZODIAC FACT

The scales is the only symbol in the zodiac that is not a living thing.

PEACEMAKERS

It is no surprise that Libras avoid arguments and disagreements. To keep the peace, they often hold back from sharing their own opinion unless they are with people they feel totally comfortable with. Making decisions is difficult for Libras, who worry about what everyone else wants. They often look to others to guide them before making up their own mind.

LIKES

◆ Fairness

◆ Being outdoors

◆ Harmony

DISLIKES

◆ Chaos or mess

LIBRA FRIENDS

While Libras enjoy their own space, they also love to socialize. Libras have a sensitive side, which makes them good listeners. They are great people to go to for advice.

COMPATIBLE SIGNS

Gemini

Sagittarius

SCHOOL REPORT

Libras enjoy learning in class and are always ready to try any other activities school has to offer, such as sports or music clubs. They will be popular with classmates and teachers.

GOOD TO KNOW

Libras like to take it easy. They are happy just watching TV, reading a book, or taking a gentle stroll in the park. They like sports but prefer to be the referee rather than a player.

SCORPIO
The Scorpion

Nothing frightens a Scorpio! This star sign is strong-willed, curious and mysterious, too. What's more, Scorpios are also resourceful and brimming with cool facts. They can win any argument—so challenge them if you dare . . .

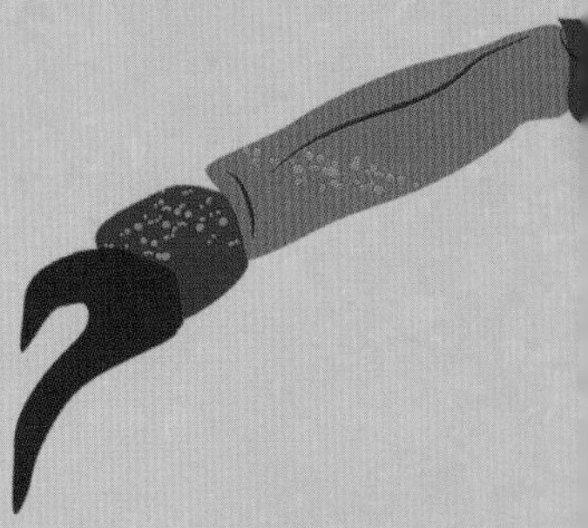

ZODIAC FACT

Scorpios are associated with three animals—the scorpion, the eagle, and the snake.

SCORPIOS ARE . . .

◆ Curious

◆ Secretive

◆ Strong

FAMOUS SCORPIOS

◆ Emma Stone

◆ Pablo Picasso

◆ Bill Gates

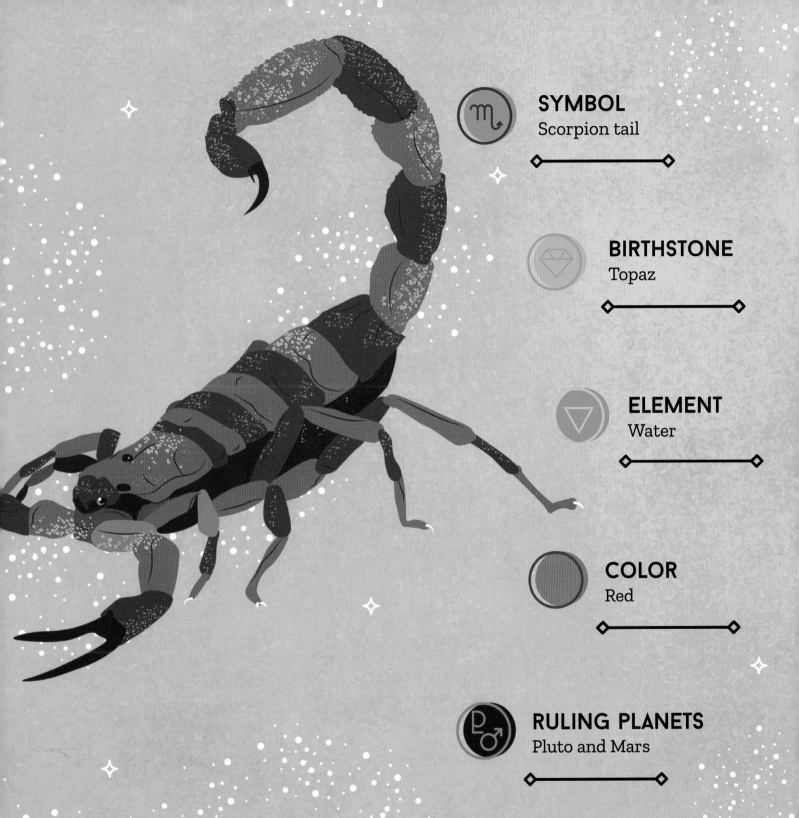

SYMBOL
Scorpion tail

BIRTHSTONE
Topaz

ELEMENT
Water

COLOR
Red

RULING PLANETS
Pluto and Mars

ALL ABOUT ♏ SCORPIO

ALL OR NOTHING

Scorpios are fierce, unflappable, and not afraid to dream big. They are determined, and will do what it takes to make their goal a reality. With their brains, this sign knows how to make things happen. Scorpios can be fiercely intelligent and use their knowledge to get what they want. Plus, they can come up with an answer to almost any problem. Scorpios are happy in the limelight as they don't often feel embarrassed!

STAR ADVICE

Learn to forgive

STING IN THE TAIL

Scorpios enjoy a good debate and they won't hold back from telling everyone how they really feel. That doesn't mean that they are entirely honest, though. Scorpios can be very secretive and won't give away their true feelings easily. Be warned, because this star sign is known for holding grudges. So, if you upset them, you had better get ready to grovel (even though you may not be aware of how you upset them in the first place!). Their secretive nature can be a bit irritating to pals who think that sharing secrets goes both ways.

LIKES

- ◇ The truth
- ◇ People with confidence
- ◇ Mysteries

DISLIKES

- ◇ Telling lies or playing mind games

COMPATIBLE SIGNS

Cancer

Taurus

ZODIAC FACT

In Greek mythology, Scorpio comes from the story of a giant man called Orion. He was described as the most handsome man there was.

SCORPIO FRIENDS

Scorpios have your back! They make loyal and protective friends. This sign likes people who are genuine, and they can spot fake friends a mile away! Building strong friendships is important for Scorpios, and they are often part of very close-knit groups.

SCHOOL REPORT

Scorpios do well in school because they are intelligent, hardworking, and determined to do their best. They love doing research for homework and will probably go above and beyond what is asked for by the teacher.

GOOD TO KNOW

Scorpios are leaders. They are strong and powerful but are also fair. Of all the signs of the zodiac, Scorpios top the league for being world leaders.

SAGITTARIUS

The Archer

Adaptable, open and friendly—these are just a few of the best qualities that describe a Sagittarius. They get a buzz exploring new places and love wandering around just to see what they come across. They also have a good sense of humor. You will definitely laugh a lot with a Sagittarius around.

ZODIAC FACT

Carnations are the flower of Sagittarius, which seems like the perfect match for this loving star sign.

SAGITTARIANS ARE ...

◆ Friendly

◆ Outgoing

◆ Curious

FAMOUS SAGITTARIANS

◆ Jay-Z

◆ Billie Eilish

◆ Billie Jean King

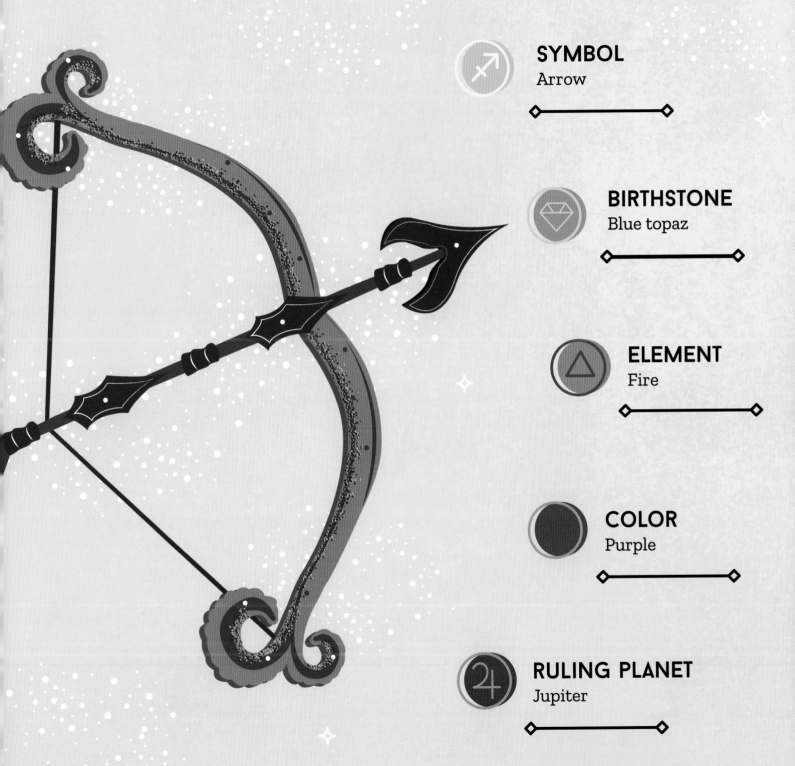

SYMBOL
Arrow

BIRTHSTONE
Blue topaz

ELEMENT
Fire

COLOR
Purple

RULING PLANET
Jupiter

ALL ABOUT SAGITTARIUS

GIVE IT A SHOT

A Sagittarius grabs just about every opportunity going. They love to go on an adventure, whether it be traveling or starting a new project. Nothing is too difficult for a Sagittarius. Team this attitude with boundless optimism and a big heart, and you've got one exciting person. Sagittarians are brutally honest. Their blunt approach can be welcome, as they tell it as it is. They will always find ways to turn their dreams into reality.

TO THE POINT

Is there a downside to all that optimism and go-getting? Besides being totally tired from their nonstop life, this sign can come across as boastful. Sagittarians can be impatient with those who take life slower than them, so they often go out on their own. Their honesty can come across as just rude, and this can upset more sensitive people. They sometimes don't see (or don't want to see) the problems in a situation, which can cause issues later on.

STAR ADVICE

Think before you speak

LIKES

◆ Being outdoors

◆ Travel

◆ Freedom

DISLIKES

◆ Having to be in a certain place at a certain time

ZODIAC FACT

Sagittarius is commonly represented as a centaur. In Greek mythology, this centaur is thought to be Chiron, a wise healer.

COMPATIBLE SIGNS

Gemini

Aries

SAGITTARIUS FRIENDS

Making people laugh is important to this star sign. They are known for their fabulous sense of humor. Sagittarians are guilty of saying yes to everything, even when they know getting it all done is impossible. This over-promising can lead to disappointing people they care about.

SCHOOL REPORT

This student loves to learn and can get bored quickly if classes are not interesting enough! This curious star sign will usually be the one asking the teacher the most questions.

GOOD TO KNOW

Sagittarians are confident, outgoing, and hardworking, which is why so many are famous! They have good self-esteem and get along well with others.

CAPRICORN

The Goat

Meet the ambitious, steady and logical star sign, Capricorn. Do you have a job that needs to be done? You can count on a Capricorn to get it done right. They are brilliant problem solvers, which is probably why they love a good puzzle!

CAPRICORNS ARE ...

◆ Independent

◆ Practical

◆ Clear thinkers

FAMOUS CAPRICORNS

◆ Greta Thunberg

◆ Martin Luther King, Jr.

◆ Michelle Obama

ZODIAC FACT

Capricorn's lucky numbers are 6, 8 and 9.

SYMBOL
Head of a goat with
the tail of a fish

BIRTHSTONE
Garnet

ELEMENT
Earth

COLORS
Brown and black

RULING PLANET
Saturn

ALL ABOUT
♑ CAPRICORN

GOAT THE JOB DONE

If you're looking for a trustworthy person, a Capricorn is a good place to start. They excel in practical tasks so, for a Capricorn, crafting and model-making is certainly no chore! They have amazing willpower, so they are the best person to have around if you are trying to achieve a goal. They won't give up if it is something they truly believe in. Capricorns are also sensitive, and are aware of their own feelings, as well as those of the people around them. You can definitely depend on people with this star sign, and they are as generous with presents as they are with their time and skills.

STAR ADVICE

Have a laugh!

ARE YOU KIDDING?

Capricorns are always on the go and they don't find it easy to let go or relax. They are stubborn and can be guilty of taking life too seriously. Although they spend a lot of time helping out people around them, Capricorns struggle to be open about their emotions and they can be over-sensitive.

LIKES

◆ Practical projects and DIY

◆ Making money

◆ Puzzles and games

DISLIKES

◆ Being silly when you could be doing something useful!

CAPRICORN FRIENDS

Capricorns take their friendships very seriously. They truly care about their pals and always want the best for them. They are always there to give support and to listen and share.

COMPATIBLE SIGNS

Virgo

Taurus

SCHOOL REPORT

Capricorns love to please people, so they will always do their best in class. They love to solve problems, so they may be good at math and science. They also enjoy sports and team games.

ZODIAC FACT

Capricorns are one of the most hardworking signs in the zodiac.

GOOD TO KNOW

Capricorns can be quite secretive themselves, so they are very good at keeping other people's secrets.

AQUARIUS

The Water Carrier

Strong-minded and oozing with confidence, Aquarians always speak their minds. They are original, quirky, and not afraid to be different. People with this star sign rarely worry about small things—they have much bigger things to think about!

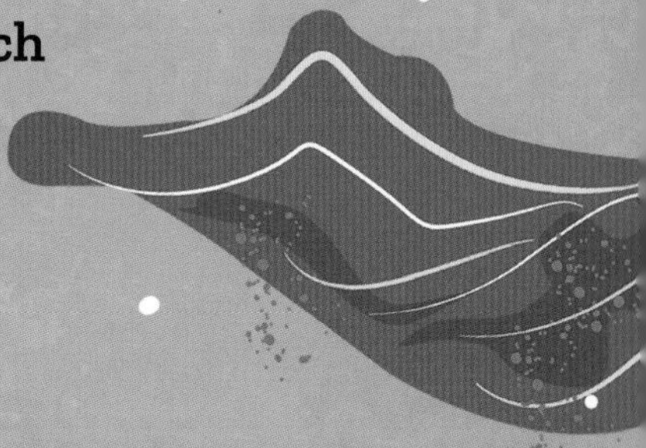

ZODIAC FACT

The colors associated with Aquarius can help you feel less stressed.

AQUARIANS ARE ...

- ◆ Tech savvy
- ◆ Strong
- ◆ Original

FAMOUS AQUARIANS

- ◆ Michael B. Jordan
- ◆ Ellen DeGeneres
- ◆ Ed Sheeran

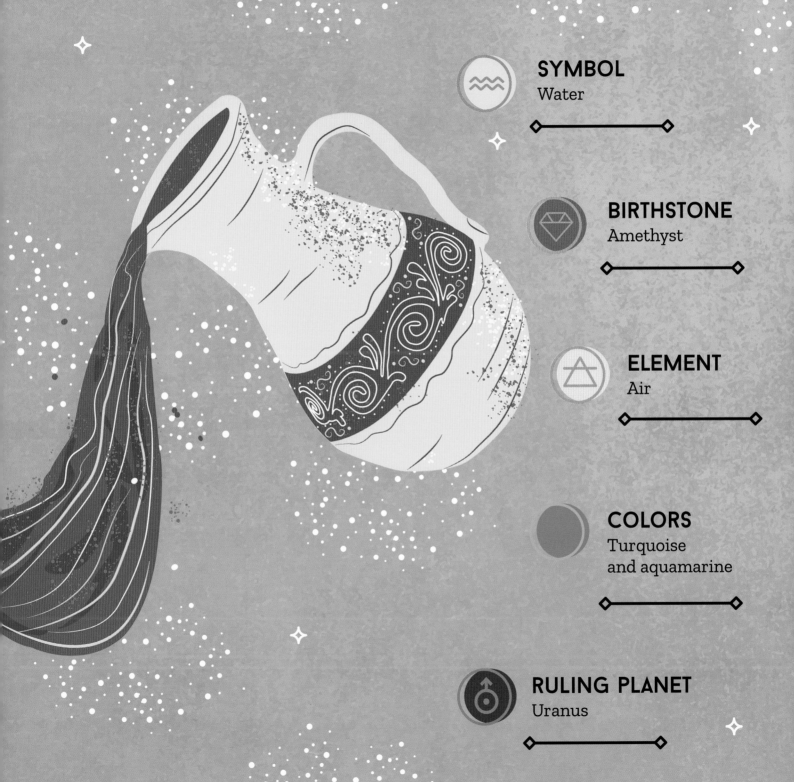

SYMBOL
Water

BIRTHSTONE
Amethyst

ELEMENT
Air

COLORS
Turquoise
and aquamarine

RULING PLANET
Uranus

ALL ABOUT
~ AQUARIUS

MAKING WAVES

Aquarians love making their own rules and going their own way in life. They are strong characters, so they tell rather than ask. One of their strongest attributes is the way that they're able to bring less confident friends out of their shell. They care deeply about the things they believe in and have the ability to make people think differently about life. Their enthusiasm makes them fun to have around!

GO AGAINST THE TIDE

Although they can be calm, Aquarians aren't people who go with the flow and will always have their own opinions. This can be a good thing, but not if you're hanging out with a big group—imagine trying to pick a movie! Aquarians are more than happy to put their foot down, and this can make them seem bossy. This shouldn't bother an Aquarius, though, as they are perfectly comfortable spending time on their own.

STAR ADVICE

Listen to others

LIKES

- ◇ Science fiction
- ◇ Writing
- ◇ Technology

DISLIKES

- ◇ Following the crowd—they like to stand out!

COMPATIBLE SIGNS

Sagittarius   Aries

GOOD TO KNOW

Aquarians are fiercely independent and happy being by themselves. They would prefer to go on a solo adventure that they can control, rather than have to follow a group.

AQUARIUS FRIENDS

This star sign is a natural leader of the pack. Luckily for them, they are so confident that others are happy to follow them. This sign is the most likely to set the trends, as they are not afraid to stand out.

SCHOOL REPORT

Aquarians want to be treated as equals, so they may not like it when teachers tell them what to do. They believe in fair play, so they will always fight bullies and stand up for people being picked on in class.

ZODIAC FACT

Their ruling planet is Uranus, which is all about shaking things up and making changes.

PISCES

The Fish

Everyone likes Pisces! They are known for their kindness and easygoing nature, so it's no surprise that this sign is popular. Pisces are sensitive folk with a real awareness of other people's feelings, and they rarely upset anyone.

PISCES ARE ...

◆ Artistic

◆ Generous

◆ Popular

FAMOUS PISCES

◆ Justin Bieber

◆ Ansel Elgort

◆ Simone Biles

ZODIAC FACT

Being able to see the good in everyone means that Pisces have a real mix of friends with different opinions and personalities.

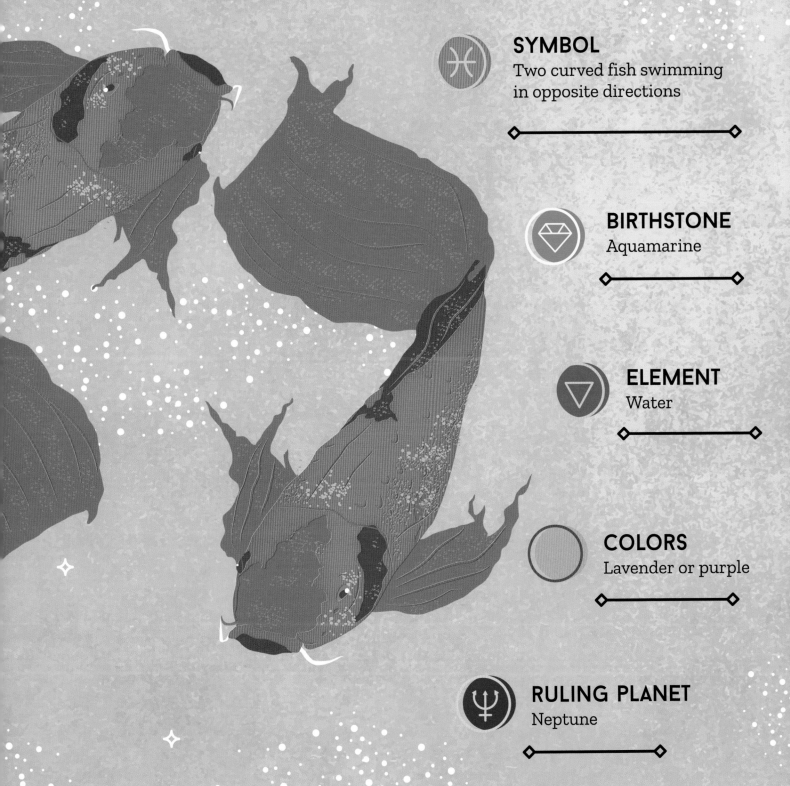

SYMBOL
Two curved fish swimming in opposite directions

BIRTHSTONE
Aquamarine

ELEMENT
Water

COLORS
Lavender or purple

RULING PLANET
Neptune

ALL ABOUT ♓ PISCES

NOT SHELLFISH

Pisces are loving, caring, and totally unselfish, which means they are often part of large social groups. These faithful friends always look for the best in people, even when they have to search really hard! Pisces can pick up on people's behavior, even if it is not obvious, which makes them great at keeping the peace if their friends are arguing.

STAR ADVICE

Stand up for yourself

ZODIAC FACT

Thursday is a lucky day for Pisces.

KIND SOLE

Loving unconditionally and always seeing the positive means that Pisces may be taken for granted by those who want to take advantage of their good nature. Pisces can get caught up in their own feelings about things and can fail to see a situation for what it really is. Their love for escaping reality means they risk putting off the important stuff. Why spend hours studying for a test when you could be reading instead?

LIKES

◇ Alone time

◇ Music

◇ Sleep

DISLIKES

◇ Being told to hurry up!

PISCES FRIENDS

Pisces tend to give everyone the benefit of the doubt. They are non-judgmental when it comes to meeting new people. Their open hearts and minds mean that Pisces are likely to have a wide circle of friends.

COMPATIBLE SIGNS

Scorpio   Taurus

GOOD TO KNOW

Pisces have a great imagination and are very creative, so they make fantastic artists, whether it is writing, painting, putting on a play, or playing an instrument.

CONSTELLATION

Pisces is a water sign with two fish as its symbol. Did you notice how the fish are swimming in opposite directions? This symbolizes the way that Pisces are always split between the real world and a fantasy one.

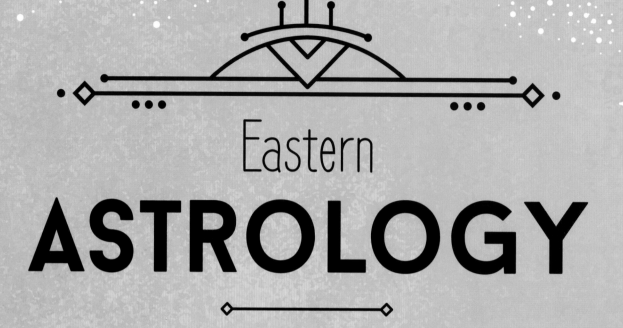

Eastern
ASTROLOGY

We have explored Western astrology, but there are a lot of different Eastern astrologies, such as Hindu or Vedic astrology and Tibetan astrology. Each form of astrology has its own way of looking at the future. One of the most popular Eastern astrologies is the Chinese zodiac. This is based on a 12-year cycle and each year has a different animal. Find your birth year in the chart to see what animal you are.

ZODIAC FACT

The cycle lasts 12 years. This is roughly the length of Jupiter's orbit around the Sun.

ZODIAC FACT

The Chinese zodiac begins at the start of the Chinese New Year, which is between January and February.

To find the signs for any years not listed on this chart, count clockwise from the latest year for future dates and counterclockwise from the earliest year for past dates.

The **Rat** comes first in the cycle!

YOUR
Chinese Zodiac

Just as in Western astrology, each of the animals in the Chinese zodiac has its own set of characteristics. Now that you know your year, read on to see how you compare to your animal.

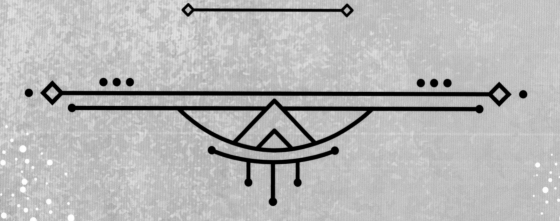

RAT

Strengths: You can try your hand at anything. Optimistic, multi-talented, and fast—nothing gets past you! Being super adaptable and organized helps make whatever you do a success.

Weakness: Can be stubborn

Compatibility: Rat or Dragon

Luck: 2 and 3 are your lucky numbers

OX

Strengths: The Ox is trustworthy and reliable. This sign is not afraid to make decisions, as they have loads of confidence and self-belief.

Weakness: They are not very open to change and dislike anyone breaking the rules

Compatibility: Rooster or Snake

TIGER

Strengths: Tigers are adventurous, kind, and strong. They aren't afraid to push themselves when faced with a challenge, either.

Weakness: Unpredictable

Compatibility: Pig or Dog

Luck: Green and blue are lucky colors

RABBIT

Strengths: Rabbits are alert, kind, and patient. As polite folk, Rabbits are also sociable and thoughtful, too.

Weakness: They can be insecure, so they appreciate a lot of reassurance

Compatibility: Pig or Goat

Luck: Red and pink are lucky colors

DRAGON

Strengths: This sign is known for being smart, hardworking, and dedicated. Dragons thrive when they receive lots of love and support from those around them.

Weakness: Can be stubborn

Compatibility: Roosters

Luck: Gold and silver are lucky colors

SNAKE

Strengths: Intelligent, funny, and brave. If there's an awkward moment, you can rely on Snakes to drop in a joke!

Weakness: Jealousy

Compatibility: Pig or Tiger

Luck: Amethyst is their lucky stone

HORSE

Strengths: Horses are energetic, kind, and independent. They love freedom! They are good at communicating, so they can easily talk people into doing what they want.

Weakness: Can struggle to make a decision

Compatibility: Goat or Tiger

Luck: Crystals are lucky for them

GOAT

Strengths: Goats are often shy. You can rely on Goats to be peacemakers, as they dislike anger. They are also very organized.

Weakness: Expecting the worst and being anxious

Compatibility: Horse or Pig

Luck: 2, 8, and 9 are some of their lucky numbers

MONKEY

Strengths: Known for their adventure-loving ways, Monkeys are funny and very competitive! These go-getters keep their cool under pressure.

Weakness: Can come across as arrogant

Compatibility: Snake or Rat

Luck: Gold and blue are their lucky colors

ROOSTER

Strengths: Courageous and clear thinkers, Roosters are excellent at making decisions. They are honest and open about sharing their opinions.

Weakness: They get into disagreements a lot

Compatibility: Dragon or Ox

Luck: 5, 7, and 8 are lucky numbers

DOG

Strengths: They are great at listening and giving advice. They are loyal and reliable and will stick by their friends through thick and thin.

Weakness: Can expect the worst in a situation

Compatibility: Rabbit or Tiger

Luck: Emerald is their lucky stone

PIG

Strengths: Gentle, kind, and loving, Pigs make great friends. They are also hardworking and like spending time with other people.

Weakness: Can struggle to concentrate

Compatibility: Tiger or Rabbit

Luck: Yellow is a lucky color

Zodiac
QUIZ

Reckon you're an expert when it comes to everything star signs?
Put your knowledge to the test with these tricky questions.

1. How long does the Chinese Astrology cycle last?

2. Which flower is linked to Leos?

3. What is the birthstone of Cancer?

4. Name the star sign that is associated with three animals (scorpion, eagle, and snake).

5. Carnations are the flower of which star sign?

6. What animal is Pisces?

7. Name the 13th constellation of the zodiac.

8. Signs are ruled by an element, but how many elements are there?

9. Which is the largest constellation in the zodiac?

10. In Greek mythology, which star sign is represented by a centaur?

Answers: 1. 12 years, **2.** Sunflower, **3.** Ruby, **4.** Scorpio, **5.** Sagittarius, **6.** Fish, **7.** Ophiuchus, **8.** Four, **9.** Hydra, **10.** Sagittarius